Fact Finders®

WHAT WENT WRONG?

The Hindenburg Explosion

CORE EVENTS OF A DISASTER IN THE AIR

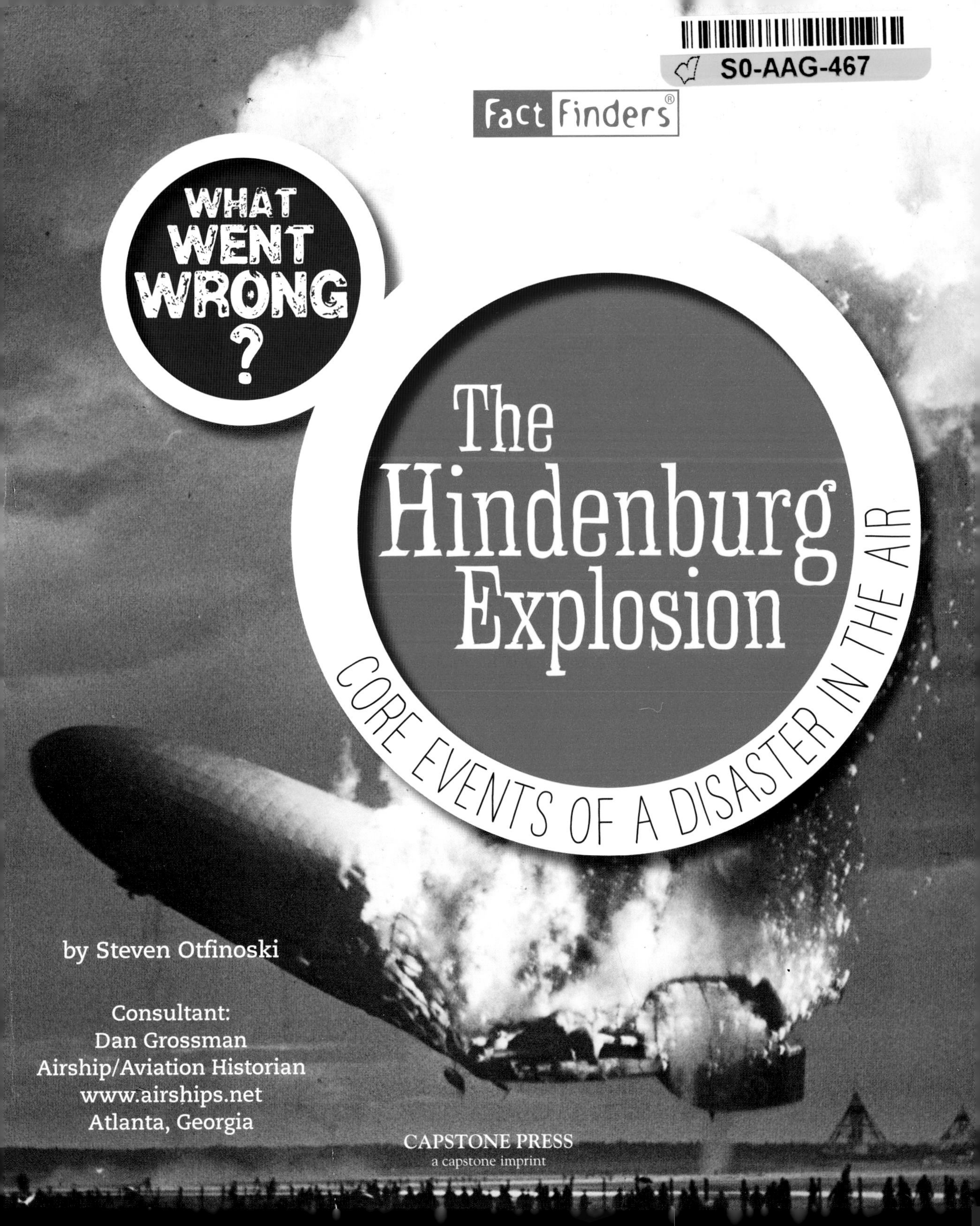

by Steven Otfinoski

Consultant:
Dan Grossman
Airship/Aviation Historian
www.airships.net
Atlanta, Georgia

CAPSTONE PRESS
a capstone imprint

Fact Finders Books are published by Capstone Press,
1710 Roe Crest Drive, North Mankato, Minnesota 56003
www.capstonepub.com

Library of Congress Cataloging-in-Publication Data
Otfinoski, Steven.
  The Hindenburg explosion: core events of a disaster in the air / by Steven Otfinoski.
    pages cm.—(Fact finders: what went wrong?)
  Includes bibliographical references and index.
  Summary: "Explains the Hindenburg disaster, including its chronology, causes, and lasting effects"—Provided by publisher.
  ISBN 978-1-4765-4184-6 (library binding)
  ISBN 978-1-4765-5133-3 (paperback)
  ISBN 978-1-4765-5982-7 (eBook PDF)
1. Hindenburg (Airship)—Juvenile literature. 2. Aircraft accidents—New Jersey—History—20th century—Juvenile literature. 3. Airships—History—Juvenile literature. 4. Airships—Germany—History—Juvenile literature. I. Title.
  TL659.H5O84 2014
  363.12'492—dc23   2013024119

Editorial Credits
Jennifer Huston, editor; Bobbie Nuytten, designer; Wanda Winch, media researcher; Kathy McColley, production specialist

Photo Credits
Alamy: DIZ Muenchen GmbH, Sueddeutsche Zeitung Photo, 7, 12-13 (top); AP Images, 10; Corbis: Christie's Images, 29, Hulton-Deutsch Collection, 23; CriaImages.com: Jay Robert Nash Collection, 14, 25; Getty Images Inc: AFP/OFF, 26–27, NY Daily News Archive, 11, 18–19, Peter Macdiarmid, 28, Time Life Pictures/Pictures Inc./Arthur Cofod, 1, 8; iStockphoto Inc: HultonArchive, 4; Library of Congress: Prints and Photographs Division, cover (left), 15, 21, 24; Mary Evans Picture Library, 17, Epic/Tallandier, 5; National Archives and Records Administration, 9; Newscom: Zuma Press/Bain News Service, 20; Shutterstock: daniana, smoke illustration, hxdbzxy, black smoke, KoQ Creative, 12 (bottom left), Leremy, 12 (bottom right), nattavut, geometric design; SuperStock Inc: Everett Collection, cover (right)

Primary source bibliography
Page 9—"Scenes from Hell." Herb Morrison, *Hindenburg* Disaster, 1937. www.archives.gov/exhibits/eyewitness/flash.php.
Page 11—"Hindenburg 75th Anniversary: An Interview with Lucy N. Holman." www.jacksonnjonline.com/2012/05/04/33007/33007/.

Printed in the United States of America.
042018 000381

In the 1930s **airships** were the most advanced form of air travel. The enormous *Hindenburg* was the grandest of them all. On May 3, 1937, the *Hindenburg* left Germany on its first transatlantic trip of the year. By that time the *Hindenburg* had already completed more than 60 successful trips. Nobody suspected that this trip would end in a **fiery** tragedy with passengers scrambling to save their lives.

A crowd gathers as the *Hindenburg* takes off on a test-flight on March 4, 1936.

Passengers enjoy a meal in the *Hindenburg's* dining area.

The "Flying Palace"

The *Hindenburg* was completed in 1936. It had taken more than four years to build. At the time it was the largest airship ever built. It was 804 feet (245 meters) long and as tall as a 13-story building. It could carry 72 passengers and a crew of 50. The *Hindenburg* had a dining room, passenger cabins, a lounge, and a writing room. People called it a "flying palace." Only the very rich could afford to fly on the *Hindenburg*. A one-way ticket cost $400—that would be more than $5,000 today!

airship—a lighter-than-air aircraft with engines and a passenger compartment hanging underneath it

fiery—like fire, or to do with fire

The *Hindenburg* had a maximum speed of 84 miles (135 kilometers) per hour. It could travel from Germany across the Atlantic Ocean to the United States in two or three days. Today the same trip would take about seven or eight hours by airplane, so two days seems like a long time. But back then airplanes weren't widely used, and it took five days or more to cross the ocean by ship. It was hoped that airships would become a safe, fast, and affordable method of transportation, much like airplanes are today. The *Hindenburg* would change all that.

Final Destination

The *Hindenburg* was running about 12 hours behind schedule on May 6, 1937. Strong winds had slowed the airship as it made its way across the Atlantic Ocean. When it finally reached its destination of Lakehurst, New Jersey, it ran into a thunderstorm. The captain steered the airship south along the Jersey shore to wait out the storm.

The *Hindenburg* returned to Lakehurst shortly after 7:00 p.m. and approached its **mooring** at the Naval Air Station. More than 200 crewmen on the ground grabbed ropes dropped from the *Hindenburg* to guide it to the mooring. On board, passengers were getting ready to leave the airship.

mooring—place where a ship (or airship) is secured, either with ropes or an anchor, to keep it from moving

A large crowd watches as the *Hindenburg* prepares to land at the Naval Air Station in Lakehurst, New Jersey.

Fire in the Sky

At 7:25 p.m. the unthinkable happened when a fire broke out in the rear of the airship. Within seconds a ball of fire rose high in the air above the *Hindenburg*. The entire airship was aflame as it floated toward the ground. Ground crew members dropped their ropes and ran for their lives.

Daring Escapes

Many people on board jumped from the airship, some falling to their deaths. Joseph Spah, an acrobat, waited until the airship was about 30 or 40 feet (9 to 12 m) from the ground. Then he jumped, hitting the ground in a roll. He walked away from the burning airship with only a broken heel.

Just seconds away from landing at Lakehurst, New Jersey, the *Hindenburg* burst into flames.

Some on board owed their lives more to luck than skill. Fourteen-year-old cabin boy Werner Franz was running to escape the blaze when he fell. At that moment, a water tank burst above him, soaking him with water. The water saved him from getting burned. He punched a hole through the side of the airship's outer covering and jumped to safety.

EYEWITNESS TO TRAGEDY

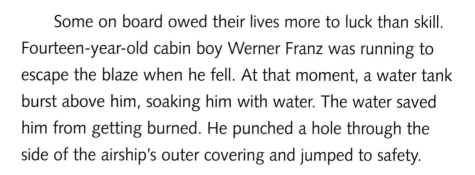

Herb Morrison, a Chicago radio announcer, was one of the newspeople on the scene to report the *Hindenburg*'s arrival. When the fire broke out, he continued his report. His emotional broadcast was one of the first times a major disaster was reported as it happened. Morrison's words have not been forgotten:

"It burst into flames ... It's crashing! ... It's burning, bursting into flames and is falling on the mooring mast ... This is the worst of the worst catastrophes in the world! Oh, it's crashing ... oh, four or five hundred feet into the sky ... it's a terrific crash, ladies and gentlemen. There's smoke, and there's flames, now, and the frame is crashing to the ground, not quite to the mooring mast. Oh, the humanity, and all the passengers screaming ..."
—Herb Morrison, reporter for WLS radio in Chicago

9

Mr. and Mrs. Otto Ernst were in the dining room when the flaming airship hit the ground. Rescuers led them safely off the airship. Otto Ernst later died from his injuries, but his wife survived. In all, 35 of the 97 people on board died, including 22 crew members and 13 passengers. One ground crew member was also killed.

People were amazed that so many people on board actually survived. Some families of survivors left the scene before learning that their loved ones were still alive. They figured that no one could have survived such a fiery disaster.

In just 34 seconds the mighty *Hindenburg* was reduced to a pile of ashes and charred ruins. But what caused the fire that brought about this terrible tragedy?

Werner Franz (front row, center) and the other surviving crew members of the ill-fated *Hindenburg*.

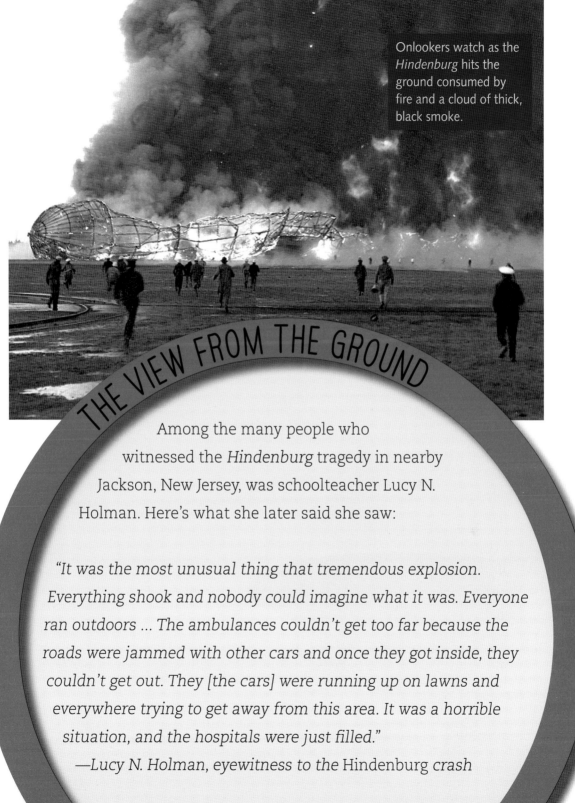

Onlookers watch as the *Hindenburg* hits the ground consumed by fire and a cloud of thick, black smoke.

THE VIEW FROM THE GROUND

Among the many people who witnessed the *Hindenburg* tragedy in nearby Jackson, New Jersey, was schoolteacher Lucy N. Holman. Here's what she later said she saw:

"It was the most unusual thing that tremendous explosion. Everything shook and nobody could imagine what it was. Everyone ran outdoors ... The ambulances couldn't get too far because the roads were jammed with other cars and once they got inside, they couldn't get out. They [the cars] were running up on lawns and everywhere trying to get away from this area. It was a horrible situation, and the hospitals were just filled."

—Lucy N. Holman, eyewitness to the Hindenburg *crash*

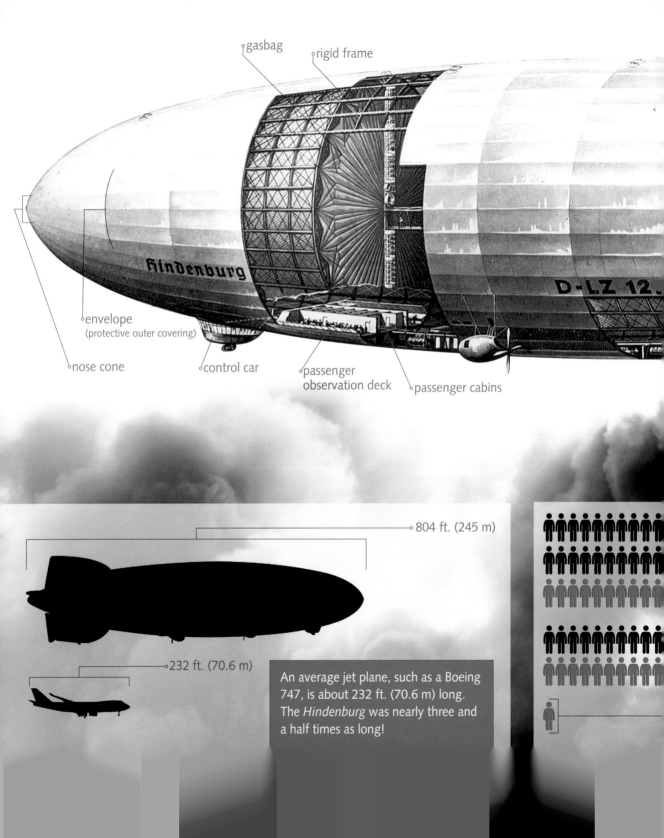

gasbag
rigid frame
envelope
(protective outer covering)
nose cone
control car
passenger
observation deck
passenger cabins

Hindenburg

D-LZ 12.

804 ft. (245 m)

232 ft. (70.6 m)

An average jet plane, such as a Boeing 747, is about 232 ft. (70.6 m) long. The *Hindenburg* was nearly three and a half times as long!

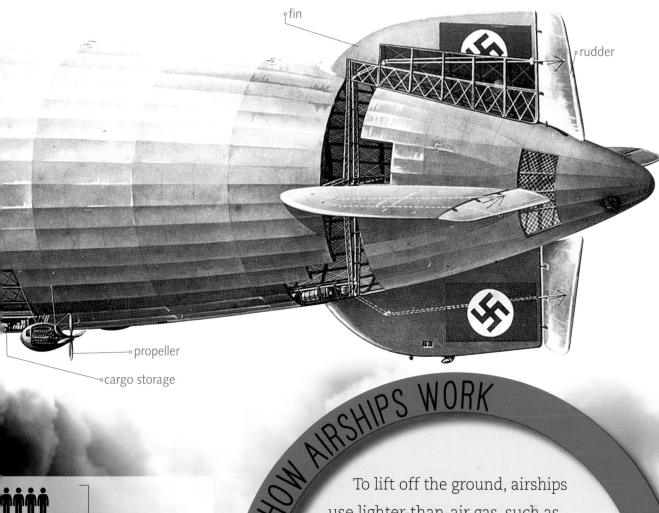

fin

rudder

propeller

cargo storage

61 crew members
22 dead

36 passengers
13 dead

1 ground crew member
also died in the tragedy

HOW AIRSHIPS WORK

To lift off the ground, airships use lighter-than-air gas, such as **hydrogen** or helium. It's the same concept as a balloon filled with helium. It will take off toward the sky if it's not held down with a string or a weight. Airships contain several large gasbags that are filled with lighter-than-air gas. These gasbags are like giant balloons. Rudders help the crew steer the airship.

hydrogen—a colorless gas that is lighter than air and burns easily

CHAPTER 2
Deadly Hydrogen

What caused the *Hindenburg* to catch fire over Lakehurst, New Jersey? Some experts believe a spark caused by static electricity in the air after the storm started the fire. Others believe that an anti-**Nazi** group planted a bomb on the airship. In fact shortly before the crash, the German Embassy received a warning that "something will happen to the *Hindenburg*." However, no evidence of **sabotage** was ever discovered.

The cause of the *Hindenburg* fire remains a mystery. But there is no doubt what caught fire on the doomed airship—the highly **flammable** hydrogen gas that filled it.

Nazi—a member of the German political party led by Adolph Hitler; the Nazis ruled Germany from 1933 to 1945

sabotage—damage or destruction of property that is done on purpose

flammable—likely to catch fire

It took just 34 seconds for fire to sweep through the hydrogen-filled *Hindenburg*.

Hydrogen is lighter than air, so it helps the airship rise off the ground. But why did the Germans use dangerous hydrogen gas instead of safer helium? At the time the United States had the only **natural resources** of helium in the world. But the U.S. government refused to export helium because there was only a small supply. Government leaders also feared that the gas would be used for military purposes. As a result the Germans were forced to use hydrogen.

In 1900 Germany's Count Ferdinand von Zeppelin invented one of the first successful airships. He called it a **zeppelin**, after himself. Much like hot-air balloons, which had been around since the late 1700s, airships were filled with lighter-than-air gas. A **gondola** on the bottom of the airship could carry many people. Airships were powered by engines that made them move speedily across the sky. Unlike hot-air balloons, airships also had steering equipment and fins that allowed them to move in any direction the pilot wanted to go.

natural resource—something in nature that people use, such as coal and trees

zeppelin—a large, oval-shaped airship with a rigid frame; zeppelins are named for their inventor, Count Ferdinand von Zeppelin

gondola—a compartment underneath a hot-air balloon or an airship

15

In 1930 another airship—the British *R101*—was filled with hydrogen when it crashed and then burst into flames in France. Hugo Eckener, the head of the Zeppelin Company, did not want this to happen to his airships. He was so determined to prevent fires on board that he did not allow people to bring lighters or matches.

Therefore, experts believe the *Hindenburg* fire was probably due to a small leak in one of the 16 gasbags. In fact, for several minutes before the airship attempted to land, the tail end (where the fire started) was sagging. Experts believe this shows that the *Hindenburg* was leaking hydrogen.

So how did the gas **ignite**? When an airship travels through the air—especially during stormy conditions—it collects thousands of volts of static electricity. It is similar to the static electricity created when rubbing a balloon on hair. Experts believe that static electricity in the air created a spark, which ignited the leaking hydrogen and started the fire.

FASCINATING FACT

Despite Eckener's concern about fires on his airships, smoking was allowed on the *Hindenburg* in a special lounge. The room was **pressurized** to prevent hydrogen from entering it. Smokers also had to use a special electric lighter that was provided for them.

ignite—to catch fire

pressurize—to seal off an area so that the air pressure inside is the same as at Earth's surface

The British airship *R101* was making its first commercial flight when it crashed in France.

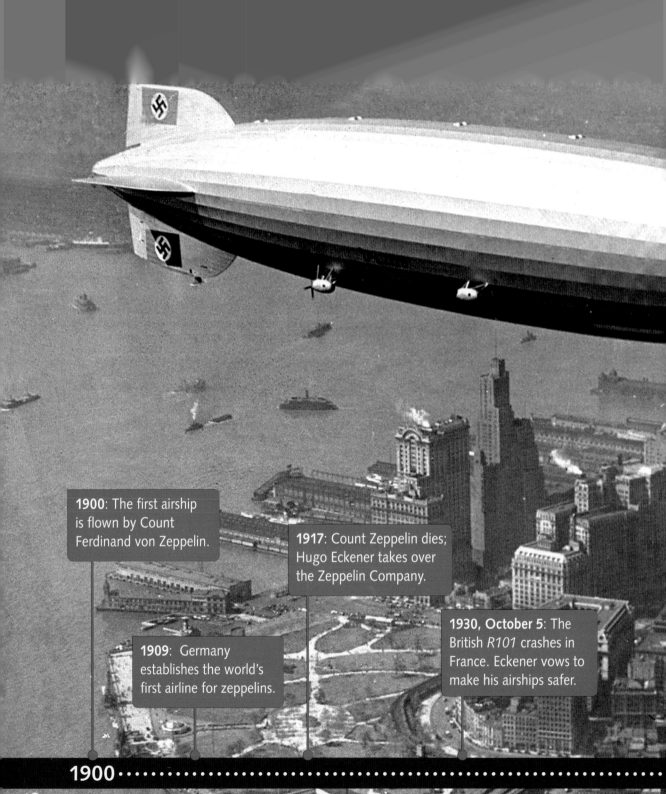

1900: The first airship is flown by Count Ferdinand von Zeppelin.

1909: Germany establishes the world's first airline for zeppelins.

1917: Count Zeppelin dies; Hugo Eckener takes over the Zeppelin Company.

1930, October 5: The British *R101* crashes in France. Eckener vows to make his airships safer.

1900

1937, May 6, 7:00 p.m.: The *Hindenburg* approaches its destination at the Naval Air Station in Lakehurst, New Jersey.

1937, May 3: The *Hindenburg* leaves Frankfurt, Germany, on a transatlantic flight.

1937, May 6, 7:25 p.m.: The *Hindenburg* bursts into flames, killing 36 people.

1936, March 4: The *Hindenburg*, the world's largest airship, is launched. It goes on to have more than 60 successful flights.

1940: The *LZ-127* and *LZ-130* are melted down to build German warplanes.

1940

19

CHAPTER 3

Tragedies in the Sky

The *Hindenburg* tragedy was one of the last airship disasters, but it definitely wasn't the first. In terms of loss of life, fewer people died in the *Hindenburg* tragedy compared to some other deadly airship disasters. But it is the most well known.

Germany's *LZ-14* and *LZ-18*

Germany had other airship disasters before the *Hindenburg*. On September 9, 1913, the *LZ-14* was on a mission for the German Navy high above the North Sea. The zeppelin had only been in the air about an hour when it encountered a storm with strong winds. Before the captain could land the airship, it crashed into the sea. Fourteen crew members drowned. The *LZ-14* was the eighth zeppelin to crash in seven years. It was one of the first airship disasters to take multiple lives.

The *LZ-18* exploded in the air and crashed outside Berlin, Germany, killing 28 members of the German Navy.

Just a few weeks later, on October 17, 1913, Germany's *LZ-18* was on a test flight when hydrogen was sucked into the engine. This set the airship on fire and caused it to explode about 10 miles (16 km) southeast of Berlin. All 28 men on board died.

Members of the German military sift through the remains of the *LZ-18*.

Katastrophe des Marine - Luftschiffes L. II
17. Oktober 1913
Phot. Gebr. Ha
Berlin

British *R101*

At 777 feet (237 m) in length, the *R101* was the largest airship ever built until the *Hindenburg* came along. On October 4, 1930, the *R101* set out on its very first overseas flight from England to India. Due to strong winds, those on the airship were in for a bumpy ride.

Around 2:00 a.m. on October 5, the *R101* was flying over France about 1,500 feet (457 m) off the ground. It was cruising along at about 38 miles (61 km) per hour. Suddenly, the airship began quickly losing speed and **altitude**. Within minutes the *R101* fell to the earth nose first. It crashed in a forest and burst into flames. Of the 54 people on board, 48 died. After the crash, the British ended their airship program.

altitude—how high a place is above sea level

The outer covering of the *R101* was completely destroyed in the crash, but the metal frame remained mostly intact.

FASCINATING FACT

After the crash of the British *R101*, the Zeppelin Company purchased some of the wreckage. Some of the metal from the *R101* was used to build the *Hindenburg*.

23

USS *Akron*

From 1925 to 1935, three U.S. Navy airships crashed in bad weather. One of them was the USS *Akron*, a vessel built in Ohio. On the night of April 3, 1933, the *Akron* left the Naval Air Station in Lakehurst, New Jersey. This was the same naval base where the *Hindenburg* was attempting to land when it crashed. Shortly after midnight on April 4, the *Akron* ran into strong winds, just like the *R101*. As the airship tried to climb higher and gain altitude in the windy conditions, the airship's tail hit the water. That caused the *Akron* to crash into the Atlantic Ocean. Seventy-three men were killed. Three lone survivors were rescued at sea.

The USS *Akron* hovers over the Goodyear docking station in Akron, Ohio.

These airship tragedies were all very similar to the *Hindenburg* disaster, but most of them resulted in more deaths. So why are they not as well remembered as the *Hindenburg*? The reason is simple. The horrific fate of the *Hindenburg* was captured on film, in photographs, and on radio broadcasts for the entire world to see and hear.

The wreckage of the USS *Akron* is recovered after it crashed into the Atlantic Ocean.

Despite the many deadly disasters during the airship's golden age (1900–1937), airships made thousands of successful journeys. These lighter-than-air vessels logged millions of miles transporting several thousand civilians and members of the military. Germany even operated the world's first passenger airline using its zeppelins.

But the *Hindenburg* disaster was seen around the world in newsreel films and photographs, and the world was horrified. After the tragedy, people were convinced that airships were unsafe for travel. Two days after the *Hindenburg* went down, the *LZ-127*, another passenger zeppelin, returned to Germany from Brazil and was grounded.

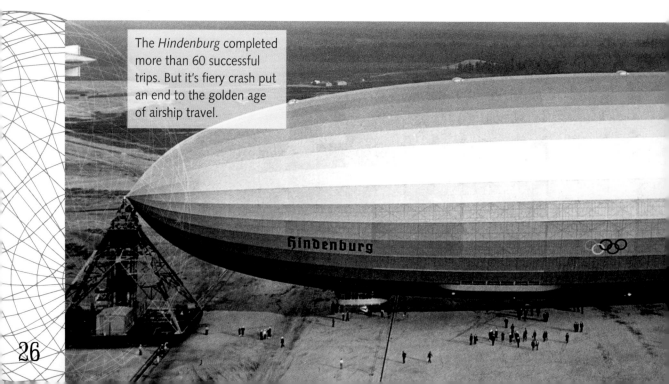

The *Hindenburg* completed more than 60 successful trips. But it's fiery crash put an end to the golden age of airship travel.

The golden age of the airship ended with the *Hindenburg*'s destruction. But airships did not entirely disappear. Although the problem with airships seemed to be hydrogen, the United States did not agree to start exporting helium. Without an effective solution to the problem, the Germans continued to use hydrogen in their airships.

In 1938 Germany's *LZ-130* flew around England on a spying mission. A year later, England and Germany were at war with each other in World War II (1939–1945). In 1940 the metal frames of the *LZ-127* and the *LZ-130* were melted down and used to build military aircraft. The United States also used airships during World War II to patrol coastal waters and to escort ships.

With the decline of airships, the popularity of airplane travel soared. Airplanes did not use highly explosive gases. They were kept in the air by wings, propellers, and powerful engines. In time airplanes grew safer and larger and were soon flying passengers all over the world.

In some countries people can take tours in modern, helium-filled airships.

FASCINATING FACT

Some buildings had docking stations where airships could land. One was built atop the Empire State Building in New York City. It was only used once by a small, private airship.

The Future for Airships

Today airships are used mainly for advertising. They are often seen over sports stadiums with ads painted on their sides. They are also used to mount TV cameras filming sporting events from the air.

In Germany anyone can take a ride in an airship. New technology makes the helium-filled zeppelins much safer than earlier hydrogen-filled ones. Zeppelin tours take passengers about 1,000 feet (305 m) in the air, offering them spectacular views of the German countryside.

As the world rediscovers this unique and imaginative form of aircraft, more uses may be on the way. In the future, airships may be used in rescue missions and heavy-lifting operations. They may even make a comeback in the travel industry. With the use of safer helium, the threat of another fiery disaster like the *Hindenburg* is less likely to occur. With the rising cost of airplane fuel, airship travel may someday become an effective and environmentally friendly way to travel.

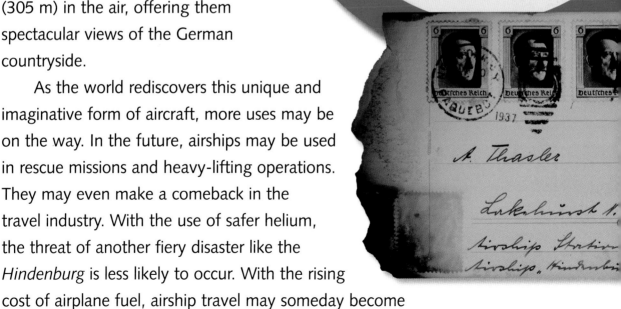

29

Glossary

airship (AIR-ship)—a lighter-than-air aircraft with engines and a passenger compartment hanging underneath it

altitude (AL-ti-tood)—how high a place is above sea level

fiery (FYE-ree)—like fire, or to do with fire

flammable (FLA-muh-buhl)—likely to catch fire

gondola (GON-duh-luh)—a compartment underneath a hot-air balloon or an airship

hydrogen (HYE-druh-juhn)—a colorless gas that is lighter than air and burns easily

ignite (ig-NITE)—to catch fire

mooring (MOR-ing)—place where a ship (or airship) is secured, either with ropes or an anchor, to keep it from moving

natural resource (NACH-ur-uhl REE-sorss)—something in nature that people use, such as coal and trees

Nazi (NOT-see)—a member of the German political party led by Adolph Hitler; the Nazis ruled Germany from 1933 to 1945

pressurize (PRESH-uh-rize)—to seal off an area so that the air pressure inside is the same as at Earth's surface

sabotage (SAB-uh-tahzh)—damage or destruction of property that is done on purpose

zeppelin (ZEP-lin)—a large, oval-shaped airship with a rigid frame; zeppelins are named for their inventor, Count Ferdinand von Zeppelin

Internet Sites

FactHound offers a safe, fun way to find Internet sites related to this book. All of the sites on FactHound have been researched by our staff.

Here's all you do:

Visit *www.facthound.com*

Type in this code: 9781476541846

Check out projects, games and lots more at
www.capstonekids.com

Critical Thinking Using the Common Core

1. How did hydrogen gas contribute to the *Hindenburg* disaster, and why did the Germans use it? (Key Ideas and Details)

2. There were other deadly airship disasters before the *Hindenburg* tragedy, some of them with higher death counts. Why was this one remembered most vividly? (Integration of Knowledge and Ideas)

3. How do the events described in the timeline show the rise and fall of the great zeppelins? (Craft and Structure)

Read More

Benoit, Peter. *The Hindenburg Disaster*. True Books. New York: Children's Press, 2011.

Graham, Ian. *You Wouldn't Want to Be on the Hindenburg!: A Transatlantic Trip You'd Rather Skip*. New York: Franklin Watts, 2009.

Gunderson, Jessica. *Fire in the Sky: A Tale of the Hindenburg Explosion*. Graphic Flash. Mankato, Minn., Stone Arch Books, 2009.

Lace, William W. *The Hindenburg Disaster of 1937*. Great Historic Disasters. New York: Chelsea House Publishers, 2008.

Verstraete, Larry. *Surviving the Hindenburg*. Ann Arbor, Mich., Sleeping Bear Press, 2012.

Index